Artist BIOGRAPHIES

Mary Cassatt

The Life of an Artist

Carolyn Casey

E | **Enslow Publishers, Inc.**
40 Industrial Road   PO Box 38
Box 398   Aldershot
Berkeley Heights, NJ 07922   Hants GU12 6BP
USA   UK
http://www.enslow.com

Mary Cassatt

Library of Congress Cataloging-in-Publication Data

Casey, Carolyn.
    Mary Cassatt : the life of an artist / Carolyn Casey.
        p. cm. – (Artist biographies)
    Summary: Discusses the life and the work of the Impressionist painter Mary Cassatt.
    ISBN 0-7660-2093-2 (hardcover : alk. paper)
    1. Cassatt, Mary, 1844–1926—Juvenile literature. 2. Artists—United States—Biography—Juvenile literature. 3. Expatriate artists—France—Biography—Juvenile literature [1. Cassatt, Mary, 1844-1926. 2. Artists. 3. Women—Biography.] I. Cassatt, Mary, 1844-1926. II. Title. III. Artist biographies (Berkeley Heights, N.J.)
    N6537.C35C37 2004
    760'.092—dc22

                                    2003017616

Printed in the United States of America

10 9 8 7 6 5 4 3 2 1

To Our Readers: We have done our best to make sure all Internet addresses in this book were active and appropriate when we went to press. However, the author and the publisher have no control over and assume no liability for the material available on those Internet sites or on other Web sites they may link to. Any comments or suggestions can be sent by e-mail to comments@enslow.com or to the address on the back cover.

Illustration Credits: Alfred Atmore Pope Collection, Archives, Hill-Stead Museum, Farmington CT, p. 42; Bibliothèque Nationale, Paris, p. 35; Carnegie Library of Pittsburgh, p. 5; Corel, pp. 6, 10, 19, 20, 26, 32; Douglas Mann/PhotoMann.com, p. 13; Giraudon/Art Resource, NY, p. 21; Library and Archives, Historical Society of Western Pennsylvania, Pittsburgh, PA, p. 9; Library of Congress, p. 38; Musee d'Orsay, Paris, France/Art Resource, NY, p. 18; National Portrait Gallery, Smithsonian Institution/Art Resource, NY, pp. 25, 33 (top); The Newark Museum/Art Resource, NY, p. 23; New York Public Library/Art Resource, NY, pp. 31, 38 (top); Private collection, Paris, France/Art Resource, NY, p. 17; Reunion des Musees Nationaux/Art Resource, NY, p. 33 (bottom); Smithsonian American Art Museum, Washington, D.C./Art Resource, NY, pp. 15, 29; Courtesy Special Collections, University of Delaware Library, p. 40.

Cover Illustration: (detail) Mary Cassatt, *Self-Portrait,* ca. 1880. National Portrait Gallery, Smithsonian Institution/Art Resource, NY

Contents

Chapter 1

Mary's Early Life

Mary Cassatt is one of the most famous women painters in history. Her paintings and pastel drawings are recognized around the world for their style. Cassatt seemed to step into the private lives of the people she painted.

Cassatt was the only American member of the French Impressionist movement, a group of artists working in the late nineteenth century. The Impressionists changed the entire world of the visual arts. But Cassatt's success came slowly, and it was a struggle.

Mary Cassatt achieved great success in her lifetime. This photo was taken in 1914, when she was seventy years old.

She had to convince even her own family to help her become a painter.

Mary Cassatt was born more than a hundred years ago. It was a time when most girls grew up

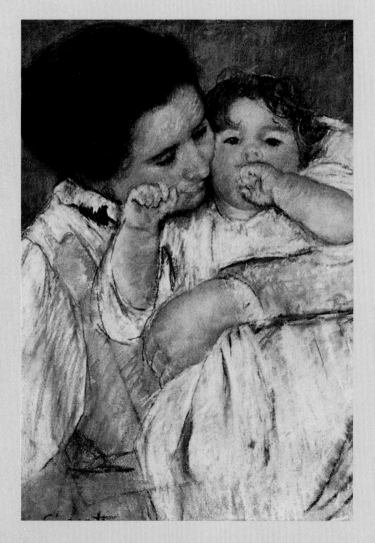

Little Anne Sucking Her Finger, Embraced by Her Mother (1897). Notice how the mother's arm completely encircles the child's body. Also notice the relaxed look on the face of the child, secure in its mother's embrace.

thinking only about getting married and raising many children. Very few women had jobs, and almost no women were professional artists.

Mary Cassatt was different. As a teenager, she decided she wanted to become a painter. She later traveled by herself all over Europe at a time when it was rare for a woman to do so. And unlike most women of that time, she never married.

From the beginning, Cassatt was determined to become famous and to paint in her own style. Rather than staying with the painting styles everyone else used, she insisted on breaking the rules. She and the other Impressionists created a brand new style of art that is much admired today.

Mary Cassatt's life was different in many ways from the life of a typical woman of the 1800s.

Chapter 2

Growing Up

Mary Stevenson Cassatt (kuh-SAHT) was born on May 22, 1844, in Allegheny City, Pennsylvania. She had one older sister, two older brothers, and one younger brother.

Mary's family lived well. They had more money than most American families at that time. Mary's father, Robert Simpson Cassatt, was a successful businessman. He and Katherine Johnston Cassatt, Mary's mother, liked going to parties and enjoyed the arts.

When Mary was seven, her parents decided to move the family to Europe. They felt their children would get a better education there than in America. They sailed across the

Atlantic Ocean and made their new home in Paris, France.

Two years later, the Cassatts moved to Germany. Sadly, while they were living there, Mary's older brother Robbie died of a bone disease in his knee that he had had for several years.

The grieving Cassatt family decided to move back to the United States. One son, Alexander, stayed behind to study in Germany.

Mary Cassatt was born in Allegheny City, Pennsylvania, not far from the city of Pittsburgh. Above is a very old photograph of the Allegheny City town hall, taken around the time Cassatt was growing up.

Jean-Auguste-Dominique Ingres, a French painter, was one of
many European masters whose works Mary Cassatt saw at the
Louvre in Paris. Ingres painted this portrait, *Madame de Sennones,*
in 1814. Notice the lady's relaxed pose and natural expression,
as well as the reflection in the mirror behind her. Similar features
can be seen in some of Cassatt's work.

Right before they left Europe, Mary and her family visited the Louvre (LOOV-ruh), a place that held the best art collection in Paris. She saw many great paintings and sculptures. The Cassatts also visited the World's Fair in Paris. Mary was amazed by some of the art she saw there.

Mary was just eleven years old when she announced that she was going to be an artist. Since there were very few women artists when Mary was a girl, this was a startling thing for her parents to hear.

In 1855, Mary's family returned to Philadelphia. Mary studied French, a language she would later speak all the time as an artist in Paris. Mary also began learning how to be a fine horseback rider. Riding horses was something she loved for the rest of her life.

Chapter 3

Learning to Be an Artist

Even though at first Mary Cassatt's parents did not like the idea of her being an artist, they helped her by paying for art classes for many years. When Cassatt was fifteen, she stopped going to her regular school. She wanted to study only art.

The next year, Cassatt convinced her parents to let her take a drawing class at the Pennsylvania Academy of the Fine Arts in Philadelphia. This art school was one of the few that allowed women to enroll. Cassatt and her best friend, Eliza Haldeman, took classes together. They visited art collections to study the styles of famous artists.

Art students often learn to paint by copying great paintings by master artists. At the Louvre in Paris and other great museums, one could usually find art students at their easels.

It is common for art students to learn to paint by making copies of famous paintings. Even as a student, Cassatt preferred to copy paintings of ordinary people rather than formal portraits of wealthy people.

As a teenager, Cassatt complained about women not being allowed to do the same things men did. But she did not let that stop her. She was determined to be a successful artist.

She stayed at the academy for four years and became very skilled as a painter. But Cassatt knew she needed to study in Paris to be successful. That was where many of the great artists lived and worked.

Cassatt's father was upset when she told the family she wanted to go to France. However, when she was twenty-one, he agreed to let her go and gave her money for the trip. Her mother traveled with her to Paris. Her friend Eliza joined her there a few months later.

Most art schools in Paris did not allow women to enroll. Those that did offered very few classes for them. But Cassatt did not give up. She and Eliza took private classes from successful painters. They went to museums to copy the works of master artists.

The famous Louvre museum became their school. Most women artists in those days did not do original work but instead sold the copies they made of famous paintings. But Cassatt made it clear to her friends that she wanted to create her own paintings.

Cassatt painted *Sara in a Green Bonnet* around 1901. Notice the lovely hint of a smile on little Sara's face.

Chapter 4

Capturing Everyday Life

After about two years, Cassatt and Eliza moved to the French countryside. They began painting villagers living their everyday lives.

Most artists in those days painted formal portraits of wealthy people. Families would dress in their finest clothes and stand stiffly for hours in their fanciest room while an artist painted them.

Mary Cassatt discovered that she preferred painting simple farmers and their families

Here is one of many Cassatt works titled simply *Mother and Child*. Cassatt shows a mother and child in close contact doing everyday activities—a common theme in her work.

Cassatt painted *Young Girl Sewing in a Garden* around 1881. Sewing was a part of most girls' everyday lives at that time.

going about their lives, raising their children, and doing ordinary things.

First she would make a quick sketch. Then she would turn the sketches into beautiful paintings. She captured images such as a mother giving her baby a bath, a farmer taking care of his animals, or people laughing together in a restaurant.

Her paintings showed movement and life. She used paint to show the natural light. Just as she had hoped, her own personal style began to develop. Some of her Paris teachers liked these unusual paintings.

At that time there was an important art show held in Paris every year. It was called the Paris Salon Art Exhibition, or "the Salon" for short. Many artists dedicated their entire year to making something the Salon judges would include in the show.

Cassatt's teachers chose one of her paintings for

In *Woman at Her Toilette* (1909), Cassatt portrays a woman looking at herself in a mirror. Notice the other mirror behind Antoinette reflecting the back of her head. We, the viewers, see her face and her reflection, but not the same view she sees of herself.

In *The Maternal Kiss,* painted around 1895, Cassatt makes the faces of a mother and child appear almost as though they are one.

the Salon, and it was accepted. It was a picture of a peasant girl playing a mandolin.

This was the first time one of Cassatt's paintings had been selected for any contest. It was unusual for the Salon judges to choose a young woman's work. It was even more unusual for them to select a work of art by an American artist.

Some people liked Cassatt's paintings from the French countryside.

But the people who judged the show said they were too informal. They said the unusual style showed Cassatt's lack of experience.

An early work of Cassatt's, *Two Women Seated by a Woodland Stream* was painted in 1869.

Painting Women and Children

Mary Cassatt was especially well known for her pictures of women with children. She often showed them doing ordinary things, such as bathing, getting dressed, or reading a book together. In some paintings, she showed the two simply sitting together, almost always tenderly touching.

The end of the nineteenth century was a time when people were just beginning to take care of children in a new way. In earlier times, children were treated as though they were small adults, without any special needs. But in Cassatt's time, many people were realizing that children needed protection, care, and lots of love. For example, laws were passed to make sure children were not forced to go to work. Many people began to understand how important it was for a child to have the love and care of a good mother.

Even though she was not a mother herself, Cassatt understood the closeness between a mother and child. Her subjects almost always look fully relaxed in their closeness. Other painters had made pictures of mothers and children, but Cassatt's pictures had a special tender and relaxed feeling that was greatly admired.

Jenny Cassatt With Her Son, Gardner, painted around 1882.

Chapter 5

A War Sends Her Home

In 1870, the Franco-Prussian war began in Europe. It was no longer safe to live in Paris. Cassatt went back to the United States, as did many other Americans.

Cassatt set up a studio in Philadelphia. She was joined there by some other American artists who had fled Europe. However, her art was unknown in America and did not sell well.

She missed the experience of being surrounded by art and artists in Europe.

Cassatt used watercolors to paint this picture of herself around 1880. You can see that *Self-Portrait* does not look at all like a photograph. Instead, it simply gives a quick impression of how Cassatt felt she looked at that moment.

Cassatt was hired to copy paintings by Correggio, an Italian master artist. The above painting, *Adoration of the Shepherds (Holy Night)*, from 1522, is an example of Correggio's work.

She tried showing some of her paintings at an art store in Chicago. But a few days after she took them there, they were burned in the Great Chicago Fire of 1871.

Also in that same year, the Catholic bishop in Pittsburgh offered Cassatt three hundred dollars to create some paintings for him. The project would involve her traveling to Parma, Italy, to paint copies of two famous religious paintings for the

26

new Saint Paul's Cathedral in Pittsburgh. This would be her first paying job as an artist.

Cassatt was eager to return to Europe. She packed her supplies and boarded a ship with her close friend, artist Emily Sartain.

The work she was copying was by an artist named Correggio. He was one of Italy's most famous painters. He had lived more than three hundred years before Cassatt was born.

In Italy, besides making the copies for the cathedral, Cassatt also created other paintings. These got a lot of attention. Her friend Emily said that everyone in Parma was talking about Cassatt's work.

One of these paintings showed people at a huge carnival. Another showed a woman following a god from Roman mythology. Cassatt blended her own ideas with what she learned from copying other artists.

Art critics in Italy and France praised Cassatt's ability to do a formal religious painting as well as a lively carnival image. An American collector bought her *During Carnival* painting for two hundred dollars. This was the first time Cassatt was paid for truly original work.

Later, she traveled from Italy to Spain. This time she traveled alone. In Spain, Cassatt painted bullfights as well as scenes from the lives of ordinary Spanish people. She also studied the works of Spanish artists, such as Velásquez and Murillo. She loved the experience. As she wrote to a friend, "I really feel as if it was intended I should be a Spaniard and quite a mistake I was born in America."

Cassatt wanted to make sure her work became known in the United States as well as in Europe. She sent her collection of Spanish paintings back to America to be shown in an exhibit.

Cassatt painted *Spanish Dancer Wearing a Lace Mantilla* in 1873 during her trip through Spain.

Chapter 6

Finding Her Style

In 1874, Cassatt returned to Paris. Her older sister, Lydia, moved there to live with her. The two women often went to the theater and opera. Mary created many paintings of women in the audience watching the shows. Her paintings showed emotion and energy. She earned money by painting portraits for wealthy tourists.

For months, Cassatt worked hard on two portraits she hoped would be chosen for the Salon. But the Salon judges would include only images that lived up to their rigid standards. Cassatt was very disappointed that only one of her paintings was accepted.

Some art critics liked her style, but others did not. Cassatt felt frustrated. It seemed to her that so many critics did not want artists to try anything new, such as painting ordinary people doing ordinary things.

One day, Cassatt saw a drawing by someone named Edgar Degas displayed in a shop window. She loved the drawing and kept returning to study Degas's style.

Before long, Cassatt and Degas met. This began a

In this print, *Woman Seated in a Loge,* from around 1881, Cassatt gave her impression of a woman at the theater looking through binoculars. Wealthy people in Paris, including Cassatt, spent many evenings at the theater.

Edgar Degas, who became a great friend to Cassatt, was most famous for his paintings of dancers. This 1878 painting by Degas is titled *L' Etoile (La Danseuse sur la Scene)*, or *The Star (Dancer on Stage)*.

friendship that lasted a lifetime. They did a great deal to help each other's careers. Late in her life, Cassatt described Degas as "the most important artist in my life."

Degas told her about a group of twenty-six painters he had joined who were experimenting with new painting styles. At that time these painters called themselves the Independents. They later came to be known as the Impressionists.

Cassatt's close friend Edgar Degas painted this portrait, *Mary Cassatt,* in the early 1880s.

Degas did this print of Cassatt and her sister around 1880 *(Mary Cassatt at the Louvre).* Notice how similar it is in style to Cassatt's Japanese-influenced print on page 38.

The Impressionists used quick brush strokes and light, bright colors. They often worked outdoors in the natural light of the sun. They wanted their art to have a spontaneous, on-the-spot feeling. They wanted to capture an impression of what they saw, with all the light and color of that exact moment.

Older, more traditional paintings had a darker look. They were more detailed and looked realistic—almost like photographs. They took much longer to make.

The new group of artists began putting on their own art shows. These shows got a lot of attention. Finally, Impressionist art was being noticed.

Degas invited Cassatt to join the new group.

"I accepted with joy," she wrote. "I hated conventional art. I began to live."

The Café de la Nouvelle Athènes in Montmartre in Paris was located across the street from Cassatt's studio. It was a popular gathering place for Impressionist artists in the 1870s and early 1880s.

Cassatt was much happier after she joined the Impressionists. In 1879, when Cassatt was thirty-four, the Impressionists had their fourth art show. She showed eleven of her paintings in it. About sixteen thousand visitors came to see the show.

Cassatt became famous after so many people saw her work. Her colors were considered very bold. Some critics liked her strong colors, but others did not.

Chapter 7

Cassatt's Career

In 1880, Cassatt made twenty-nine paintings, and her work was selling well.

At about this time, Cassatt's parents moved in with her and Lydia in Paris. Lydia had been diagnosed with a deadly kidney disease. Their parents moved to Paris to help run the household so that Cassatt could have time to paint.

She now spent a lot of time at home. Her parents often modeled for her. She was able to create portraits of their daily life that were touching, funny, and even sad.

In 1881, Lydia died. Mary was so overcome with sadness that she stopped painting for six months.

When she returned to her work, Cassatt did many paintings of mothers and their children. These were to become her most famous images.

Mary was a good friend to many artists. When she was in her forties, she helped other European artists by encouraging American collectors and museums to buy their work. People valued her opinion of other people's work.

In 1890, Cassatt saw an exhibit of Japanese wood-block prints at the École des Beaux-Arts (School of Fine Arts) in Paris. These prints featured simple scenes of everyday life in Japan using bright, bold colors. During this time, many French artists became interested in making prints in Japan's simple, clean style of art.

Cassatt decided to make prints. But rather than making prints of Japanese images as some French

Cassatt made the print called *In the Omnibus* in 1891, after seeing an exhibit of Japanese wood-block prints in Paris. Cassatt used the Japanese style but continued to portray her usual subjects—American and European women and children.

Girl with Insect Cage and Girl Reading a Letter by Kitao Shigemasa is an example of the kind of Japanese work that influenced Cassatt and many other artists in the 1890s. Notice how straight lines are used to break up the space in both images.

artists did, Cassatt chose to make prints of European women working in their homes. Her works are considered some of the most valuable prints made during that time.

In 1893, Cassatt had her first large solo show in Paris. She included about a hundred of her paintings, prints, and pastels. The show was a great success. Even the critics praised her work.

That same year, some Americans chose Cassatt to paint a huge mural for the 1893 Chicago World's Fair. Her mural would take up one entire wall of the Women's Building.

The mural was 14 feet tall and 58 feet wide. In order to work on a mural so large, Cassatt turned a large greenhouse in Bachivillers, France, into a studio. She set up pulleys to raise and lower the mural while she worked on it.

This was an important time for women in Europe and the United States. Many people were fighting for women to be given the right to vote in elections. The Women's Building at the Chicago World's Fair was an important place to show off the talents of women. One wall would show women from the past, while Cassatt's mural would show modern women.

Cassatt's mural had three separate frames. The first featured young girls in the quest for fame. In the second, young women plucked the fruits of

Shown here is *Young Women Plucking the Fruits of Knowledge* (1893), the second frame of Cassatt's mural for the Chicago World's Fair.

knowledge. In the third, women created art, music, and dance.

Many people did not like Cassatt's mural. The details were hard to see from the ground. The light colors she used did not work well on a mural. But even though the mural was considered a failure, Mary Cassatt's name finally became known in the United States. In 1895, she had a major show in New York that included many mother and child paintings. Art critics in New York admired her work.

In her sixties, Cassatt began to have health problems. It was hard for her to paint. She became more and more active in women's issues. In the early 1900s, she worked hard to help convince the U.S. government to allow women to vote.

Cassatt had many artist friends, but she also missed her family. By now, both of her parents had died. In addition, Cassatt had problems in both eyes and was losing her sight. She had surgery four times but nothing helped. She became nearly blind.

When she was seventy, Cassatt had to stop painting. During the remaining twelve years of her life, she often felt sad and frustrated. Some people said she had a bad temper.

Nevertheless, Cassatt continued to show and sell her earlier work. In 1904, France awarded Cassatt the Legion of Honor for her work as a painter. It was rare for a woman, and

In this 1903 photo, Cassatt is sitting beneath a Japanese fan painted by Degas.

especially an American, to get such an award. In 1914, the Pennsylvania Academy of the Fine Arts—Cassatt's first art school—awarded her the Gold Medal of Honor.

Cassatt died in France on June 14, 1926, when she was eighty-two years old.

Today, Cassatt's paintings are in many museums. Her work is included in most exhibits of Impressionist art. The U.S. Postal Service issued stamps in 2003 honoring four of her paintings. People still enjoy looking at her work.

Throughout her life, Mary Cassatt followed her own dreams. She challenged people's views of what women could accomplish and ignored those who tried to discourage her.

Long after her death, Mary Cassatt continues to inspire artists and art lovers all over the world.

Timeline

1844 Born Mary Stevenson Cassatt on May 22 in Allegheny City, Pennsylvania.

1851 Family moves to Europe for four years.

1865 Moves on her own to Paris to study art.

1868 Is honored by having one of her paintings selected for the Paris Salon art exhibit.

1870 Returns to Philadelphia.

1871 Travels to Parma, Italy, to make copies of Correggio paintings.

1874 Settles in Paris with her sister, Lydia.

1879 Exhibits art in the Impressionists' show.

1890 Begins creating Japanese-style prints.

1893 Has first large solo show in Paris. Paints mural for Chicago World's Fair.

1904 Awarded France's Legion of Honor.

1926 Dies in France on June 14 at age eighty-two.

Words to Know

art critics — People who are considered experts in art, who judge art, write about it, and help decide how valuable it is.

formal — Stiff and fancy, not carefree.

original — Completely new; never seen before.

pastel — Type of crayon that artists use.

professional — Earning money by doing something, as opposed to just doing it for fun.

rigid — Not able to bend or change.

spontaneous — Happening right at one particular moment without advance planning.

visual arts — Works of art that can be displayed in a room for people to look at, such as drawings, paintings, and sculpture.

wood-block prints — Type of art made by carving a picture into a wood block, then putting paint or ink on the block and pressing the block onto paper to create an image. The same block can be used again and again.

Mary Cassatt

Internet Addresses

The best way to learn more about any artist, including Mary Cassatt, is to see the art—the real thing, not just photographs of it. That is easy if you happen to live in a large city with a large art museum, such as Philadelphia or Chicago. But if you do not, try the Internet. The Web sites for Cassatt listed on the next page were written for people of all ages, so the text may be a bit too hard for you to get through. That is okay, though—you are just visiting for the pictures.

WebMuseum, Paris: Mary Cassatt shows about fifteen of Cassatt's paintings, including several of mothers and children. It also has links to other Impressionist artists.

http://www.ibiblio.org/wm/paint/auth/cassatt

The National Gallery of Art includes an online "tour" of about twelve of Cassatt's Japanese-influenced prints. On each page, you see one of the works and get information about Cassatt's life.

http://www.nga.gov/collection/gallery/cassatt/cassatt-main1.html

Artcyclopedia, The Fine Art Search Engine: Mary Cassatt has numerous links to Cassatt paintings that are displayed on the Web sites of various museums. This site also has links to articles about Cassatt and her work.

http://www.artcyclopedia.com/artists/cassatt_mary.html

Index